The AniMilliner's ALPHABET

a book of animals
and their hats
from around the world

by **Ed Pokoj**

Copyright © 2020 by Ed Pokoj.

Published by Zazu Zine + Comix, P.O. Box 635, Prince George, VA 23875.
www.zazuzine.com
Contact at kwe@kwepub.com.

ISBN (hardback) 978-1-950306-29-9

First Edition.

All rights reserved. No part of this publication may be reproduced in any means, electronic or mechanical, including recording, photocopying, or any information storage or retrieval system, without written permission of the author. Although every precaution has been taken to verify the accuracy of the information contained herein, the author assumes no responsibility for any errors or omissions. The author shall have neither liability nor responsibility to any person or entity with respect to loss or damage caused, or alleged to have been caused, directly or indirectly, by the information contained in this book.

This book is typeset in Garamond Premier Pro.
The illustrations were created in ink with digital colors.

This book is dedicated to my parents and grandparents.
Thank you for fostering my imagination and creativity.
Also, thank you for buying me more hats
than any one kid really needs.

Hello and welcome to the AniMilliner's ALPHABET! What is an AniMilliner you ask? Well first we ought to start with what a Milliner is. A Milliner is someone who makes and sells hats for women. An AniMilliner therefore is someone who makes and sells hats for animals. It makes perfect sense! What animals wear hats you ask? Well just go ahead and turn the page and you will find out!

A is for an Abyssinian Cat wearing an Atef

The Abyssinian Cat is one breed of cat that can be found in Egypt, a country whose ancient culture thought cats were sacred, or very special. Speaking of sacred, the Atef is the crown of the Egyptian god Osiris.

B is for a British Bulldog wearing a Bowler

The British Bulldog is from England, where the bowler hat was first worn to protect one's head from tree branches while riding on a horse.

C is for a Coyote wearing a Campaign Hat

The Coyote is prevelant in Canada where members of the Royal Canadian Mounted Police, or Mounties, wear Campaign hats as a part of their uniform.

D is for a Dandie Dinmont Terrier wearing a Deerstalker

The Dandie Dinmont Terrier is a small dog that is native to Scotland. Who is also native to Scotland? With a little detective work, one will find that Sir Arthur Conan Doyle, the creator of Sherlock Holmes, was born in Edinburgh, Scotland. Holmes is often depicted wearing a deerstalker.

E is for a European Hare wearing a Eugenie Hat

The Eugenie Hat is named for Empress Eugenie, the wife of Napolean III and the last empress of France, who was originally from Spain. One can also find the European Hare throughout Spain.

F is for a Fennec Fox wearing a Fez

The Fennec Fox is a small-bodied, big-eared, type of fox that can be found in Morocco. The Fez is named for the city of Fez which was the former capital of the Kingdom of Morocco.

G is for a Garden Dormouse wearing a Gibus

The Garden Dormouse can be found throughout France. In 1840 in Paris, France, Antoine Gibus perfected the collapsible opera hat. This type of hat has been called the Gibus ever since.

H is for a Harbor Seal wearing a Hard Hat

The Harbor Seal can be found basking in the California sun of San Francisco Bay area. The Golden Gate Bridge, which spans the stretch between the bay and the Pacific Ocean, was the first construction site to be deemed a "Hard Hat Area."

I is for an Impala wearing an Isicholo

The Impala runs through the plains of Africa at speeds of up to 55 miles per hour. They run in a zig-zag pattern like those found on some Isicholos, the traditional Zulu headresses for married women.

J is for a Jaguar wearing a Jipijapa

Jipijapa is not just the name for this woven palm hat, but also the name of the town in Ecuador where these hats are made and the name for the palms that the hats are made from. The Jaguar prowls the coasts of Ecuador.

K is for a Kingfisher wearing a Kufi

Pronounced: Koo-Fee

The Kingfisher, in many varieties, can be seen flying in the skies of West Africa, where the Kufi is a traditional hat worn by men.

L is for a Lynx wearing a Lika Cap

The Lika Cap has been a part of traditional dress in Croatia since the Battle of Krbava Field in 1493 when the Croats chased out the Turks. Even though Croatia boasts the largest population of Lynx in the world, the large cat's population is only between 40 and 60 in Croatia.

M is for a Mink wearing a Mortarboard

The Mink can be seen scurrying about in the wilderness of Massachusetts. One can also find Harvard, the USA's first university, in Boston, Massachusetts. Harvard was founded 140 years before the USA, in 1636.

N is for a Naja Kaouthia wearing a Ngob

Pronounced: Nay-jah Cow-oo-thee-uh & Nn-gahb

The Ngob is the traditional hat of the farmers of Thailand, shielding them from the sun and the rain. The Naja Kaouthia or Monocled Cobra, one of the most venomous snakes in the world, is also found in Thailand.

O is for an Osprey wearing an Ochipok

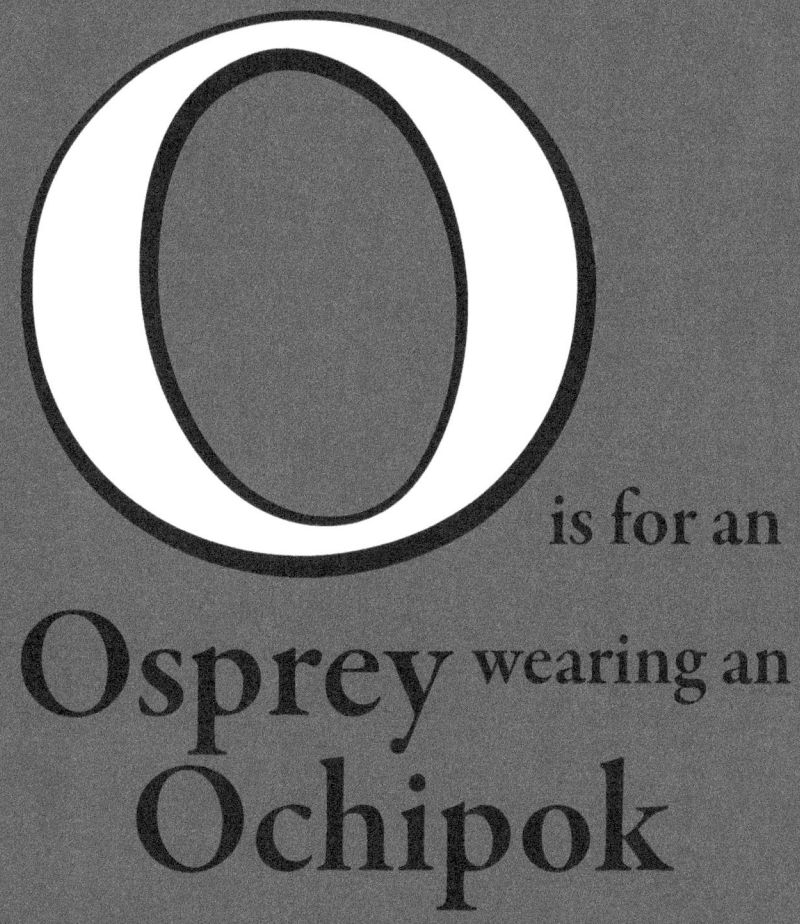

Pronounced: Oh-chih-pock

The Ochipok is the traditional headdress of married women in Ukraine. The headdress is often decorated with Ukrainian embroidery and patterns. The Osprey can also be found in Ukraine, where hunting birds of prey is banned.

P is for a Pigeon wearing a Pork Pie Hat

Pigeons can be found throughout the world, including Hollywood, California, where Buster Keaton famously wore the Pork Pie Hat in the early days of cinema.

Q is for a Qīngwā wearing a Qing Guanmao

Pronounced: Ching-wah & Ching Gwaan-maow

The Qing Guanmao was the hat worn by officials in Qing Dynasty China. Qīngwā means green frog in Mandarin Chinese.

R is for a Roe Deer wearing a Rogatywka

Pronounced: Roga-tifka

The Rogatywka is a four pointed hat that is worn as part of the Polish military uniform. The Roe Deer can be seen roaming throughout Poland.

S is for a
Southern Flying Squirrel
wearing a Stovepipe Hat

Southern Flying Squirrels glide and leap from tree to tree in the state of Kentucky, where the Stovepipe Hat's most famous wearer, President Abraham Lincoln, was born.

T is for a
Tawny Owl wearing a Tiara

The Tawny Owl soars regally over Greece, where the tiara has been worn for centuries as a symbol of royalty and victory at formal occassions.

U is for a Ussuri Brown Bear wearing an Ushanka

Pronounced: Oo-soo-ree & Oo-shon-kah

The Ussuri Brown Bear can be seen roaming the far eastern regions of Russia. In their cold winters, Russians wear warm fur Ushankas to keep their heads warm.

V is for a Velvet Purple Coronet wearing a Vueltiao

Pronounced: Vool-she-ow

The Vueltiao is a traditional handmade hat of Colombia. The Velvet Purple Coronet, a type of hummingbird, can be seen in Colombia fluttering from flower to flower.

W is for a Woodpecker wearing a Whoopee Cap

Even though New York City is so large, it is home to many types of woodpeckers. New York City is also where the Archie Comics character Jughead Jones, who wears a Whoopee Cap, was created.

X is for an X-ray Tetra wearing an X-ray Protective Cap

X-ray Protective Caps are worn by doctors and nurses to protect against negative effects of radiation. However, you don't need radiation to see the insides of the X-ray Tetra. This fish is almost entirely see through already. (Unfortunately this one couldn't be connected through geography... I just couldn't see it.)

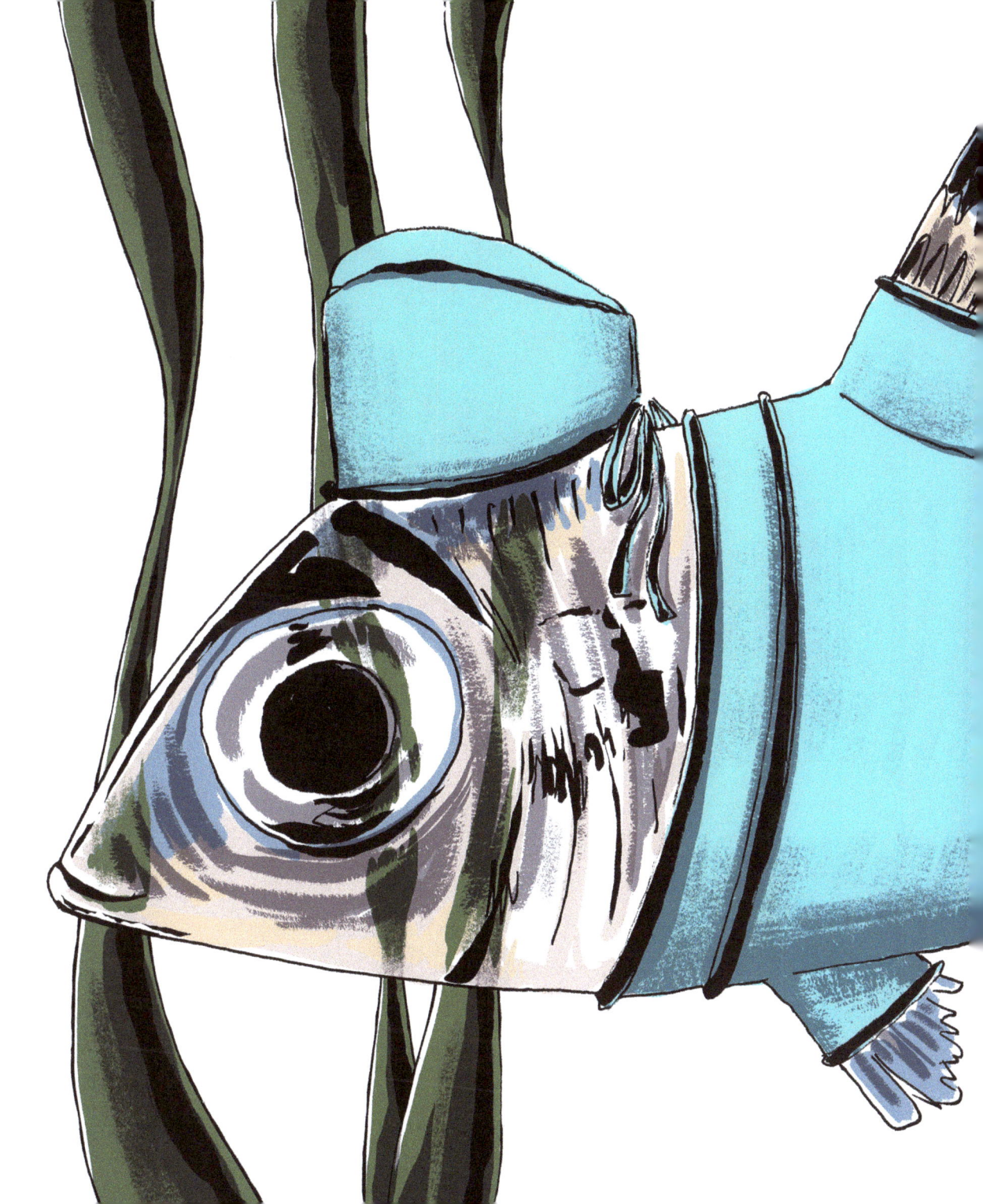

Y is for a Yellowhammer wearing a Yarmulke

Pronounced: Yaa-muh-kuh

The Yarmulke is a cap traditionally worn by Jewish men. Israel, declared an independent state in 1948 and the Jewish homeland, is also in the path of the Yellowhammer's migration.

Z is for a Ziege wearing a Zischägge

Pronounced: Zee-geh & Zish-ah-geh
The Zischägge was commonly worn by soldiers in the 1600s in Europe, specifically in Germany, where a goat is called a Ziege.

About the Author

Ed Pokoj was born in Buffalo, NY. Buffalo was Ed's home from his birth through his high school years, during which he attended St. Joseph's Collegiate Institute. It was here that Ed made his decision to pursue the arts professionally, undoubtedly because of the encouragement he received from his family, friends, and teachers. Ed moved to Richmond, Virginia in 2011 to study graphic design at VCU... where he changed paths and studied animation, video art, and sound design. After a semester abroad in Bristol, England, studying stop-motion animation, Ed returned to Richmond where he lives to this day.

Ed Pokoj is an illustrator, animator, and puppet creator. He can really best be described as a visual storyteller. He has been working in illustration since 2015. With inspiration drawn from classic kids books and comic art to stop motion animation and music. In 2017 he illustrated his first children's picture book, *What Does A Princess Really Look Like?* by Mark Loewen, as well as the coloring book that went along with it. Music, and his caffeinated buddy Ajay Brewer, inspired him to create two Hip-Hop-themed coloring books and a gallery show at The Well Art Gallery in Richmond, Virginia. He also had the opportunity to work on projects that have been of the larger variety; a mural for Chapel RVA, banners with Scout Design that have been hanging in downtown Richmond since 2017, and a giant bamboo horse named *Ody The Outsider* at The Branch Museum of Architecture and Design.

For more information on Ed's work, visit *www.edpokoj.com*.

www.ingramcontent.com/pod-product-compliance
Lightning Source LLC
Chambersburg PA
CBHW042354280426
43661CB00095B/1043